Dear Parents and Educators,

Welcome to Penguin Young Readers! As parents and educators, you know that each child develops at his or her own pace—in terms of speech, critical thinking, and, of course, reading. Penguin Young Readers recognizes this fact. As a result, each Penguin Young Readers book is assigned a traditional easy-to-read level (1–4) as well as a Guided Reading Level (A–P). Both of these systems will help you choose the right book for your child. Please refer to the back of each book for specific leveling information. Penguin Young Readers features esteemed authors and illustrators, stories about favorite characters, fascinating nonfiction, and more!

Hedge-Hedgey-Hedgehogs

LEVEL **2**

GUIDED READING LEVEL **H**

This book is perfect for a **Progressing Reader** who:
• can figure out unknown words by using picture and context clues;
• can recognize beginning, middle, and ending sounds;
• can make and confirm predictions about what will happen in the text; and
• can distinguish between fiction and nonfiction.

Here are some **activities** you can do during and after reading this book:
• Nonfiction: Nonfiction books deal with facts and events that are real. Talk about the elements of nonfiction. On a separate sheet of paper, write down what you learned about hedgehogs.
• Sight Words: Sight words are frequently used words that readers must know just by looking at them. They are known instantly, on sight. Knowing these words helps children develop into efficient readers. As you read the story, have the child point out the sight words below.

give	live	of	put	take
just	may	once	some	think

Remember, sharing the love of reading with a child is the best gift you can give!

—Bonnie Bader, EdM
  Penguin Young Readers program

*Penguin Young Readers are leveled by independent reviewers applying the standards developed by Irene Fountas and Gay Su Pinnell in *Matching Books to Readers: Using Leveled Books in Guided Reading*, Heinemann, 1999.

To Bailey, the best pet ever!—BB

PENGUIN YOUNG READERS
An Imprint of Penguin Random House LLC

Penguin supports copyright. Copyright fuels creativity, encourages diverse voices, promotes free speech, and creates a vibrant culture. Thank you for buying an authorized edition of this book and for complying with copyright laws by not reproducing, scanning, or distributing any part of it in any form without permission. You are supporting writers and allowing Penguin to continue to publish books for every reader.

Text copyright © 2016 by Bonnie Bader. All rights reserved. Published by Penguin Young Readers, an imprint of Penguin Random House LLC, 345 Hudson Street, New York, New York 10014. Manufactured in China.

Library of Congress Cataloging-in-Publication Data is available.

ISBN 978-0-448-48974-2 (pbk)   10 9 8 7 6 5 4 3 2 1
ISBN 978-0-448-48975-9 (hc)   10 9 8 7 6 5 4 3 2 1

HEDGE-HEDGEY-HEDGEHOGS

by Bonnie Bader

Penguin Young Readers
An Imprint of Penguin Random House

Is this a ball?

Is this a rock?

No!

They are hedgehogs.

Hedgehogs are small animals.

They only weigh about

one pound.

Some people keep hedgehogs
in their gardens.
Hedgehogs like to eat pests
that live there.

A hedgehog can't see very well.

So it uses its ears to find food.

Chomp, chomp.

A snail is eating a leaf.

The hedgehog eats the snail.

A hedgehog also uses its nose
to hunt.

Sniff, sniff.

The hedgehog smells a bug.

It eats the bug in one bite.

A hedgehog can also make
a good indoor pet.
But check the laws in your town
to see if you can have one.

Be careful of your hedgehog's
sharp spines.
Put your hand under
the hedgehog.
There is fur there, not spines.

Be sure to give your hedgehog

time to get used to you.

Only hold it for

a few minutes a day.

It is not hard to take care

of a hedgehog.

It only needs about two spoons

of food a day.

You can feed your hedgehog
dry cat food.
Your hedgehog can also eat
raw or cooked meat.

A small cage makes
a good house for a hedgehog.
You can also use
a small plastic tub.

Put in a dish for food.

And a dish for water.

Or you can use a water bottle.

Put wood chips in

the bottom of the house.

Or put down paper.

You do not have to take

your hedgehog for a walk.

It will go to the bathroom

in its house.

But be sure to clean its house out

once a week!

Lick, lick.

Your hedgehog will clean itself.

Hedgehogs do not like the cold.
Be sure to put your hedgehog's
house in a warm place.

During the day, your hedgehog

will sleep curled up in a ball.

Your hedgehog will be
awake at night.

Hedgehogs like to hide.
Put something in your
hedgehog's cage that
it can hide in.
Hedgehog, hedgehog,
where are you?

Hedgehogs like to play.

You can give your hedgehog
a wheel.

Run, run, run!

If you have a dog or cat,

be careful.

Your other pets may think

your hedgehog is a toy.

And their noses might get poked.

Hedgehogs should go
to the doctor.
Just like you do.

But your hedgehog

only needs to go

once a year.

Hedgehogs are cute.
Hedgehogs are tiny.
And hedgehogs can
make great pets!